I set out my clothes.

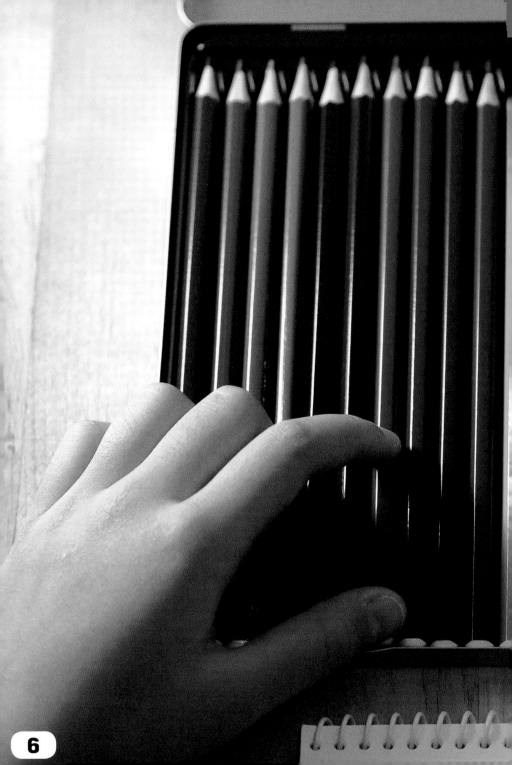

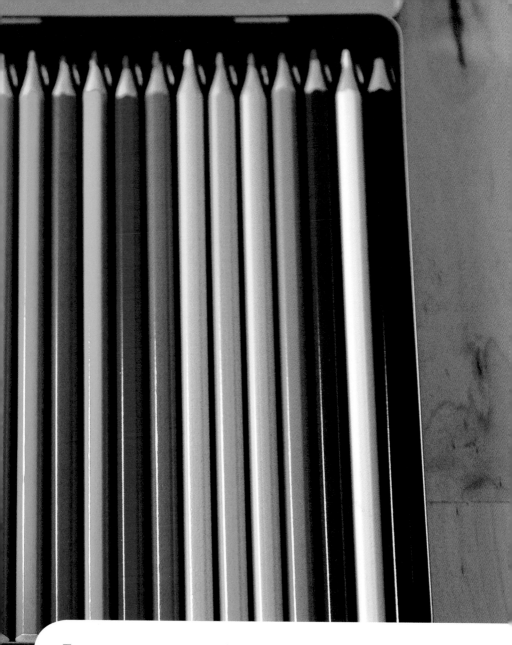

I set out my pencils.

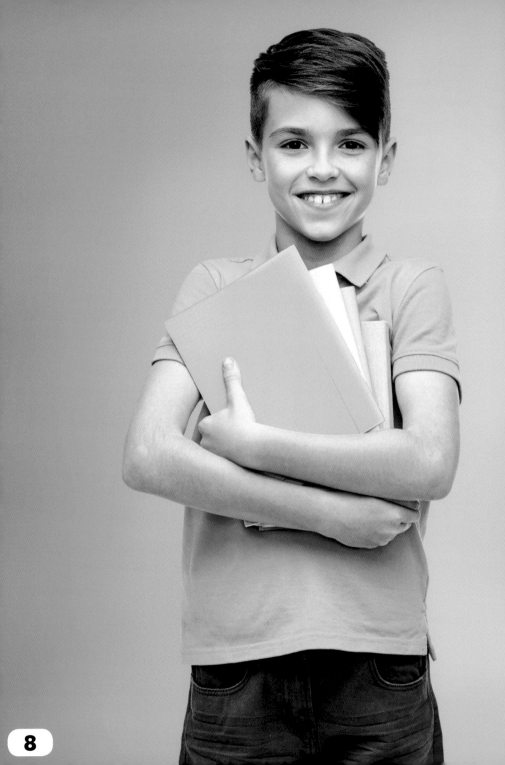

I set out my notebooks.

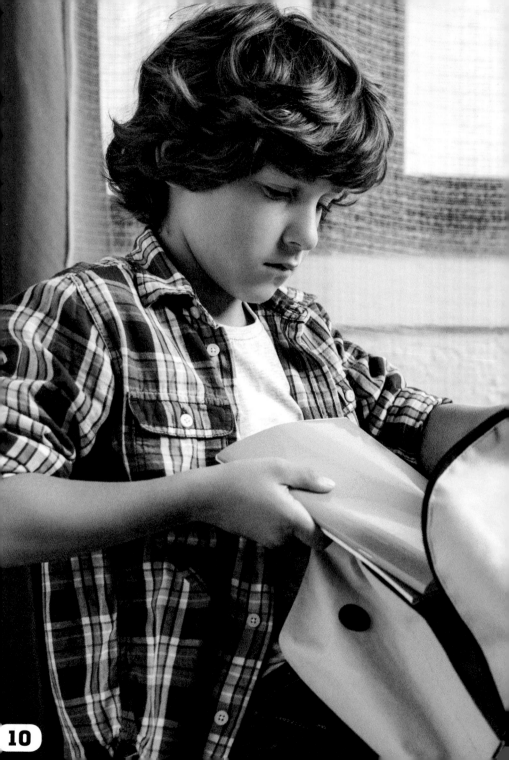

I set out my backpack.

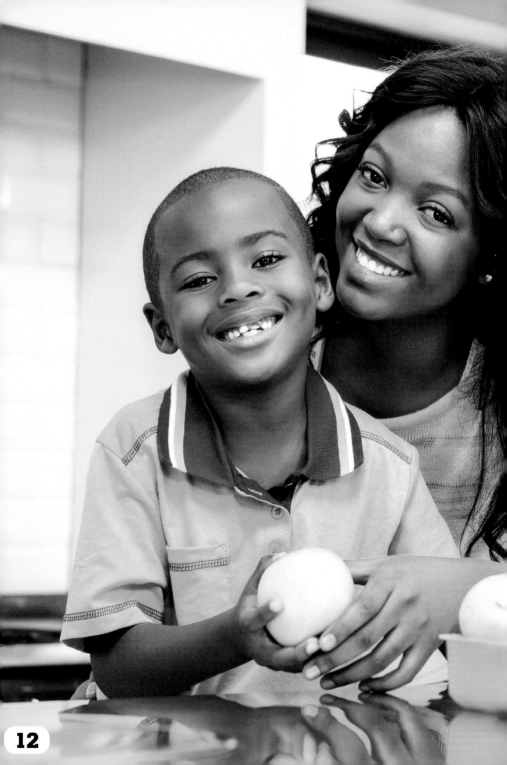

I set out my lunch box.

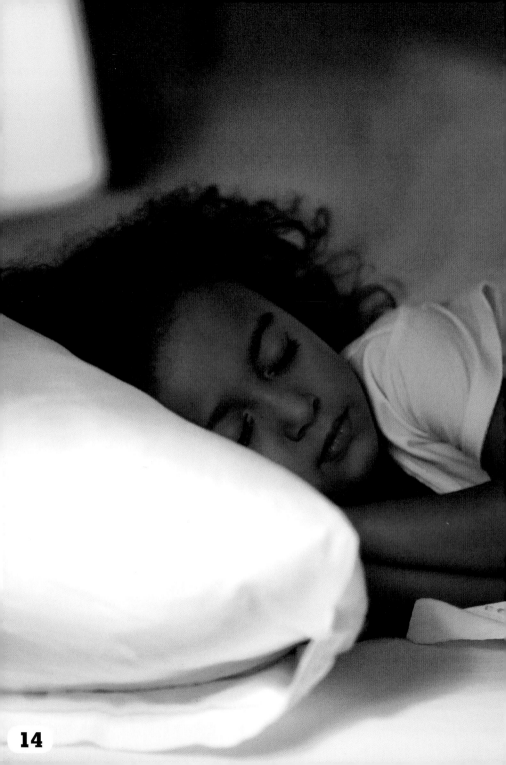

School starts tomorrow.

# What kinds of things do you make plans for?

## Did You See It?

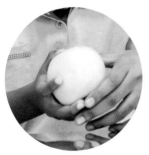

apple

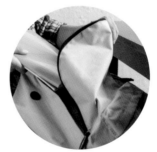

backpack

pillow

## Index